Learn Simple Serging™

Diana Cedolia

Annie's®

Why Use a Serger?

Have you ever wondered what a serger can do for you? It will streamline your sewing experience while creating professional-looking seams and hems, and decorative topstitching.

Sergers have come a long way since they were introduced to the home-sewing market in 1969. Today's machines are far more versatile in their usefulness and capability, and they make the early two- or three-thread sergers seem primitive in comparison. Depending on the brand and model, your machine may accommodate five or more threads, have special attachments and even include a computerized stitch advisor.

The basic function of a serger is really quite simple: It simultaneously sews a seam while it trims the fabric edges and encases them in neat, even stitches. And thanks to a differential feed system, which is available on most modern machines, sewing with knits is a breeze. This system consists of two feed dogs working together to evenly draw in and push out the fabric, eliminating annoying stretching and puckering.

The nine projects that are included in this book are designed to teach important basics. Most can be completed using only a serger. (However, the Ribbon Weave T-Shirt, the Take-a-Bow Tree Skirt, the Fiesta Tiered Skirt and the Stipple-Chic Clutch require a sewing machine for topstitching.)

Let's get started! As you create, you will grow to love your serger as much as I love mine.

Happy Serging!

Meet the Designer

Before discovering a serger, Diana Cedolia made clothes with a sewing machine. "No matter what I tried, from zigzagging seam edges to steam pressing hems and collars, the clothes still looked homemade." Then she bought a serger, and she never looked back. Diana began making clothing that looked as if it had come from a designer boutique, and after making a new wardrobe, she made doll clothes, linens, quilts and throw pillows. "When using a serger, all fabrics from slinky knits to crisp cottons take shape quickly and look great."

Diana lives in Florida with her husband, Pat. There she teaches hands-on serging classes, and when asked about what her students most want to make, she replied, "They want to make anything that they can finish in one or two class sessions and, luckily, sewing with a serger makes this possible. They like to learn about construction sequence and about all of the handy techniques that I have discovered over the past several years."

With her business partner, Kothy Haferstat, Diana designs quilt patterns for longarm quilting machines, and embroidery patterns for embroidery machines. The two also produce instructional DVDs for embroidery software. Their products are available under the name Simply Everything.

Table of Contents

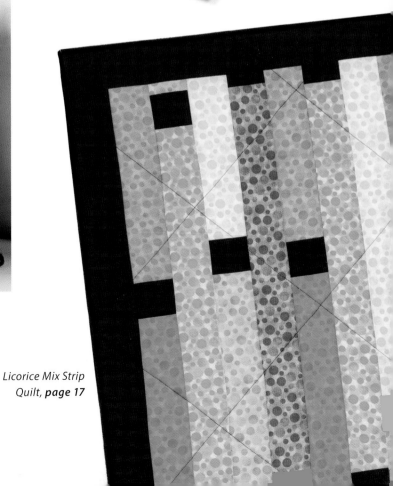

Ribbon Weave T-Shirt,
page 22

Tumbled Nine-Patch Throw Pillow, ***page 39***

*Licorice Mix Strip
Quilt,* ***page 17***

Getting Started

Knowing Your Serger

The first step in successful serging is understanding your machine's features and how to use them. Begin by locating and learning about the fundamentals of your machine. The following illustration is a generalized look at today's serger parts.

Carefully read the manufacturer's manual to familiarize yourself with each component of your serger and what its particular function is. Keep your manual nearby during project construction for easy reference.

A) **Chain Stitch Looper (Part of the Lower Looper System)**

B) **Feed Dogs**

C) **Hand Wheel**

D) **Lower Knife**

E) **Lower Looper**

F) **Lower Looper Tensions**

G) **Needles**

H) **Needle Thread Tensions**

I) **Presser Foot**

J) **Spool Holders for Thread**

K) **Thread Guide**

L) **Upper Looper Tension**

M) **Upper Knife**

N) **Upper Looper**

O) **Front Cover**

P) **Stitch Finger**

Q) **Differential Feed**

R) **Stitch Length**

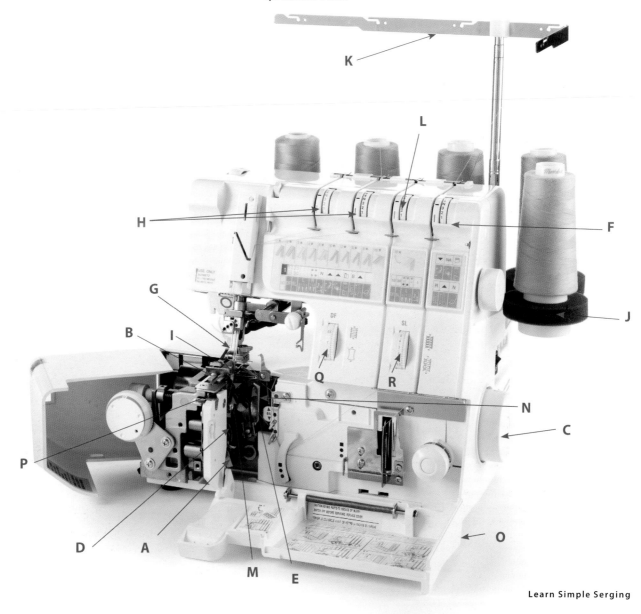

Supplies

Needles, thread, specialty feet and sewing notions—once you have the right supplies your serger will take you places you could only dream of going with a regular sewing machine.

In this section, we'll help you select the best products to use for project success. Get ready to achieve professional-looking results and to explore endless creative options!

Needles

Check your owner's manual to see if you can use conventional sewing machine needles or if your serger requires special serger needles. Selecting the correct needle for the fabric, thread and stitch type can prevent all kinds of frustration including broken needles, broken thread, holes or snags in the fabric, puckered seams and uneven stitches. Universal, ball point, embroidery and quilting are among the most popular specialty needles.

Universal Needle

Sizes/Features: 60/8 to 120/19. Slightly rounded point is rounded enough for stitching knits, yet pointed enough for stitching woven fabrics.

Use/Fabrics: General stitching on woven and knit fabrics in a wide range of weights.

Ball Point Needle

Sizes/Features: 70/10 to 100/16. Point is more rounded than universal point.

Use/Fabrics: Needle slides between yarns of knits instead of piercing them, eliminating risk of snags or holes. Good for spandex and interlock knits that run easily; also good for creating even stitches on heavy knits.

Machine Embroidery Needle

Sizes/Features: 75/10 to 90/14. Large eye and deep scarf are designed to protect thread while stitching dense designs at high speeds. The scarf is the indentation on the back of the needle that allows bobbin thread to pass smoothly through the needle's eye.

Use/Fabrics: Machine embroidery with rayon or other specialty threads. Use on any fabric finish or weight.

Quilting Needle

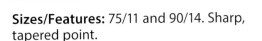

Sizes/Features: 75/11 and 90/14. Sharp, tapered point.

Use/Fabrics: Designed for stitching through multiple fabric layers and intersecting seams. Use to piece quilt tops and to quilt through multiple layers.

Threads

Serging allows for the use of a wide variety of threads. Use heavyweight thread, decorative thread or specialty serger yarns in the loopers to create embellishments that can't be duplicated with a standard sewing machine.

Selecting Threads

Quality counts when it comes to choosing threads for your serger project. Inexpensive threads may appear to be a bargain, but don't be fooled! They often fray, break, skip stitches or produce excess lint. High-quality threads will result in smooth, uniform stitches, fewer broken threads and a more attractive finished edge.

Remember that the needles will be stitching the seam and the loopers will be overcasting the edge. If you want to use heavyweight decorative threads, thread them through the loopers only and use all-purpose serger thread in the needles.

For serging seams it usually isn't necessary to purchase three or four cones of each color for a project. Instead, match the needle thread to the fabric and finish the edges with a complementary color or a neutral color, such as taupe or gray.

You may want all threads to match for rolled edges, flatlock or chain stitching. Experiment with using various types of decorative threads in interesting combinations to find the ones you like best.

For best results, use thread that is cross-wound on a cone. These threads unwind from the top without spinning, making them the best choice for feeding smoothly through the machine and for accommodating high-speed sewing. Many cotton, rayon, metallic, nylon, polyester and additional decorative threads are available on cones.

But you are not limited to threads on cones. Most sergers are built with thread adapters. If your model does not have an adapter, they are available for purchase at fabric stores and from sewing machine dealers. Thread adapters make it possible to use all shapes and sizes of spools, and even bobbins on your serger.

Accessories & Notions

Just like your sewing machine, your serger has special accessories to expand your creative options and helpful notions designed to make your life easier. The following are just a few of the many available. Check with your machine dealer or manufacturer's website for more accessories and notions.

Most serging will be done with the all-purpose serger presser foot that came with your machine. But there are specialty presser feet available for sergers just like those for your sewing machine. You will be using a gathering foot for the Fiesta Tiered

Skirt (page 34), and a piping foot for the Stipple-Chic Clutch (page 43), and Tumbled Nine-Patch Throw Pillow (page 39).

Gathering Foot

Also known as a shirring foot or separator foot, it is used for joining two pieces of fabric while gathering one of the layers as it is attached. Refer to machine manual or foot instructions on how to attach and use.

Piping Foot

This foot is available in two sizes, one for applying standard-size piping and a larger version for decorator piping. Refer to machine manual or foot instructions on how to attach and use.

Lint Brush

Use this stiff brush to keep the loopers and blades free of excess lint. Don't use compressed air for this task because it will force fine thread and fibers into the moving parts of your machine.

Choose from three different tools to secure thread chains within seams: tapestry needle, double-eye needle or loop turner.

Tapestry Needle

Insert the thread chain into the eye and slide it under the stitched seam. Trim ends.

Double-Eye Needle

Insert the thread chain into either eye and slide it under the stitched seam. Trim ends.

Loop Turner

Slide the tool under the stitched seam and grab the thread chain. Pull the thread chain under the stitched seam. Trim ends.

Seam Sealant

Ideal for securing thread ends and for preventing frayed fabric edges. Apply a small dot on the thread chain at the fabric edge. Let dry and trim the thread ends.

Thread Nets

Sergers sew rapidly! This means that threads may slip from the cone and tangle as you sew. Wrap thread nets over cones to prevent sliding, tangling and uneven feeding of thread.

Tweezers

Serger tweezers are used to grasp thread ends while threading your machine. The long tips allow for access to tight places.

Basic Sewing Supplies & Equipment

In addition to the specific supplies needed for serging, you will need the following:

- Sewing machine in good working order with zigzag or overedge stitch capability
- Matching all-purpose thread
- Hand-sewing needles and thimble
- Straight pins and pincushion
- Seam ripper
- Removable fabric marking pens or tailor's chalk
- Measuring tools
    variety clear sewing rulers
- Pattern tracing paper or cloth
- Point turner
- Pressing equipment
    steam iron and board
    press cloths
- Scissors
    fabric shears
    paper scissors
- Seam sealant

Optional Supplies & Equipment

- Fabric spray adhesive
- Rotary cutter, mats and straightedges

Stitching Basics

Unlike a sewing machine that forms stitches with a needle and bobbin, the basic serger overlock stitch is formed with needles and loopers. As the fabric is fed through the machine, the upper looper forms a loop that lies on top of the fabric, while the lower looper forms a loop that lies underneath the fabric, encasing the edge. The thread in the needle or needles catches and secures the interlocking loops to the fabric forming a straight line. They also lock at the fabric edge.

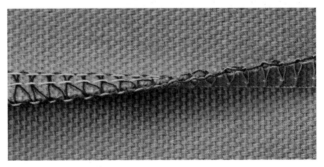

Mastering the Controls

Even if your serger has a computerized stitch advisor that shows you the exact settings for each stitch, it's important to know how the controls work and what each does so that you can make adjustments when needed. Different fabrics and threads

8

react differently to serger stitching. You will often make modifications in order to get the perfect stitch for your project. Once you get to know your serger, you won't be afraid to fine-tune the settings.

Trimming Width

One of the best time-saving features of a serger is the cutting system. It trims the fabric with two blades (one upper and one lower) that work together like scissor blades to cut the fabric. On most sergers, the upper blade can be moved out of the way for cover stitches and for some flatlock applications.

You will want to adjust the cutting width to accommodate certain fabrics or stitches, or to correct tension problems.

The distance between the upper blade and the needle closest to the blade is the cutting width, or the width of the fabric edge that will be finished with the serged stitches. It is different from the seam allowance, which is the distance between the needle and the edge of the fabric. Usually when serging seams, part of the seam allowance will be cut off. A computerized machine may have a special setting to increase or decrease the cutting width. However some basic models require that you move the blades manually. Consult your owner's manual to see if you have this option and how to use it.

Trimming Tips

• *Sharp blades are important for a clean-cut edge. Plan to replace the blades when they begin to dull. Man-made fabrics, like polyester and tricot, will dull your blades more quickly than those made from natural fibers.*

• *Some bulky or heavy-weight fabrics can be difficult to cut with your serger, even with sharp blades and a wider cutting width.*

To start a smooth cut, measure the cutting width and use scissors to cut into the first inch of the fabric edge.

This enables the feed dogs and presser foot to grab the fabric and stitch a straight seam at the beginning of the seam. It may also be necessary to sew at a slower speed.

Stitch Width

Change the needle position to alter the stitch width. Use the left needle only for a wide stitch and the right needle only for a narrow stitch. Consult your machine manual to see if it has additional controls to make this adjustment.

You can also adjust the stitch width by moving the stitch finger. The stitch finger is located on the throat plate and acts as a mini-knitting needle to form loops (Figure 1).

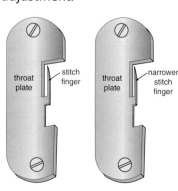

throat plate — stitch finger

throat plate — narrower stitch finger

Figure 1

Depending on your model, there will be a lever to adjust the stitch finger, or you may need to move it manually. Consult your owner's manual to learn how to move the stitch finger.

Stitch Length

Like sewing machine stitches, the length of serger stitches can be adjusted. Simply set the stitch length on your machine as you would for a sewing machine. A normal overlock stitch length is 2.5mm (3⁄32 inch) on medium-weight woven fabric. Decrease the length for lightweight fabrics and/or fine threads and increase it for heavy-weight fabrics and/or thick threads.

Decreased length

Increased length

Differential Feed & Presser-Foot Settings

A differential feed system has two sets of feed dogs with one in front of the other. The front set of feed dogs guides the fabric under the presser foot and the back set feeds it to the back of the serger. When you adjust the differential feed system, the front set of feed dogs will feed more or less fabric under the front foot. Modified feeding evenly gathers the fabric to create a ruffle or stretches it to create a lettuce leaf edge.

Check your manual for specifics on adjusting the differential feed system. On most machines, the fabric is gathered as the differential feed number is increased and stretched as the number is decreased.

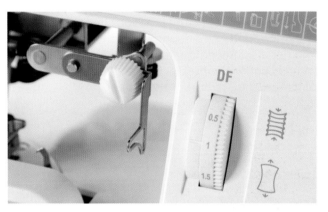

If your serger does not have a differential feed system, you can compensate for fabric weight and stretch by adjusting the presser foot pressure. A lighter pressure will allow thick and/or stretchy fabric to pass easily between the feed dogs and presser foot, leaving a smooth seam. Refer to your owner's manual for more information.

Threading Basics

Don't panic when threading or rethreading your serger. It is more complicated than threading your sewing machine, but it is a task you can easily master. It is important to note that the loopers and needles must be threaded in the correct order for the machine to stitch properly.

Some models can be threaded in any order, and a few can even thread themselves, but most machines specify to thread the upper loopers first, then the lower loopers, then the needles. Refer to your owner's manual and note the recommended sequence. Incorrect threading will result in crossed threads that will break or jam when you begin stitching.

Use serger tweezers as needed to help position the threads as you guide them through each looper and needle. It is also important to place all threads under and behind the presser foot before you begin stitching to ensure that your first few stitches are embedded in the fabric correctly. The loopers and needles move simultaneously. Anchor all threads under the presser foot or they will pop out of the needle eye and/or the looper.

Threading Tip

Make sure the threads are placed securely between the plates in the tension guides. If they are misplaced, the stitched seams will incorrectly indicate that the tension needs adjusting.

Don't despair when it is time to rethread. Practice rethreading so you will be prepared when you break a thread or when you change the thread color. If you are changing colors it isn't necessary to completely rethread the machine. You can "tie on" the new thread to the strand that is already in place.

Clip the thread close to the cone and place the new color on the thread stand (Figure 2).

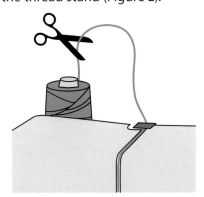

Figure 2

Tie the new thread to the end of the old thread with a tight square knot, leaving 2- to 3-inch tails on the knot (Figure 3).

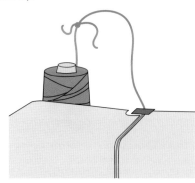

Figure 3

Adjust the tension to zero, and slowly and carefully pull the thread through the guides. Knotted thread can be drawn through the looper but not the needle. Attempting to do so will bend or break the needle. When the knot reaches the needle, cut it from the strand and insert the end into the eye.

If a break requires you to rethread, it is important to note that the threads must be replaced in the correct order. For example, if the looper thread breaks, the needle threads must be removed before rethreading the looper. Refer to your owner's manual for your model and note the recommended sequence.

Thread Identification Tip

To gain a better understanding of the threading system, use a different color of thread for each needle and looper. When you stitch a sample seam, you will see which thread came from which spool and where it appears within the embedded seam. This will help with tension adjustments because you can easily identify the problem looper and/or needle.

Tension Basics

After improper threading, improper tension is the cause of most stitching irregularities. As with threading, once you understand how it works, it is easier to make the correct adjustments. When the looper and needle threads all form an even stitch, the tension is referred to as being "balanced."

Tension is affected by fabric weight and thread weight. Test the stitch on a scrap of the project fabric before beginning. Once you have perfected the stitch, you can begin your project with confidence.

On a balanced 3- or 4-thread overlock, the upper looper threads form an "S" shape on the top of the fabric and lock with the lower looper thread along the fabric edge. The lower looper thread forms a "V" for 3-thread stitching or a "Y" for 4-thread stitching. The "V" or "Y" will appear on the underside of the fabric and lock with the upper looper thread along the fabric edge.

Balanced 4-Thread Overlock

Adjusting Tension

Looper tension that is too tight or too loose will cause seams to appear unbalanced. The upper looper tension is too tight if the stitches are pulling the lower looper thread to the top of the fabric. Experiment with adjustments until the stitch is balanced.

Upper looper tension is too tight.

The lower looper tension is too tight if the stitches are pulling the upper looper thread to the underside of the fabric. Experiment with adjustments until the stitch is balanced.

Lower looper tension is too tight.

Additional tension problems with an overlock seam can include looper tension that is too loose, and needle tension that is too tight or too loose. Refer to your owner's manual for complete instructions for creating a balanced seam.

Adjusting Tension on a Rolled Edge

Balanced rolled edge

The upper and/or lower looper tension is too tight if the stitches sit on the fabric surface without wrapping the edge. Make tension adjustments to achieve an evenly rolled edge.

The needle tension is too loose if the thread forms loops on the underside of the fabric and the edge lies flat. Make tension adjustments to achieve an evenly rolled edge.

Stitch Primer

The stitches you can make with your serger depend on the number of threads it is capable of using at the same time. Refer to your machine owner's manual to set up stitches. Before beginning your project, always test your stitches on fabric that is similar to the project fabric to perfect them.

The projects in this book are made with a combination of the following stitches. Check the Serger Stitches list in each pattern to see which stitches are being used to make the project.

4-Thread Overlock

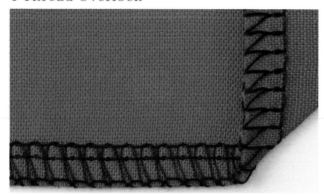

The 4-thread overlock is the most popular stitch on a serger. It is created by using both needles and both loopers. Because it produces a strong seam with two lines of needle stitches, it is ideal for construction of garments and home decor projects. It also makes an attractive and sturdy finished edge.

3-Thread Overlock

Because it uses only one needle and both loopers, the 3-thread overlock has more stretch and is lighter weight than a 4-thread overlock. It is ideal for seams that don't need the reinforcement of a second line of needle stitches. Like the 4-thread overlock, it makes an attractive finished edge.

3-Thread Rolled Edge

The rolled edge is a simple stitch that is used to create decorative edges. It works best with soft and lightweight fabrics. The tension for the lower looper thread is tightened to pull the upper looper thread snuggly around the fabric edge causing it to roll slightly. This technique cuts, folds and evenly wraps the edge.

2-Thread Flatlock

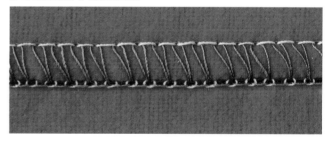

A flatlock seam is formed with one needle and the upper looper only. The needle tension is loosened to allow the stitch loops to extend beyond the folded edge (Figure 4). When the fabric is unfolded, the loops form perpendicular stitches.

Fabric

Figure 4

Chain Stitch

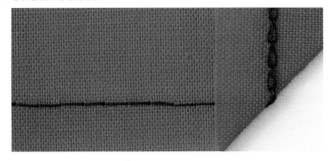

Made with one needle and one looper, a chain stitch can be used for seams or for decorative stitching. A straight stitch appears on the right side of the fabric, and a chain stitch on the wrong side. This stitch is very easy to remove by pulling the looper thread to unravel the seam.

Cover Stitch

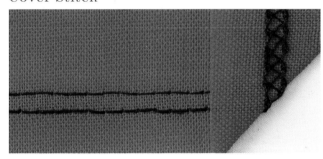

This stitch has the most stretch of any serger stitch. The cover stitch has two parallel rows of topstitching on the right side of the fabric, and decorative stitching on the wrong side. Made with two needles and one looper, it is often seen on ready-to-wear knit clothing.

Serging Seams

For most fabrics, pins aren't necessary to secure layers. If you do need to use pins, insert them away from the seam line and remove them before they reach the blades. Running over a pin with your blade will seriously damage the blade.

Begin stitching by inserting the fabric under the toe of the foot. The feed dogs will grab and pull the fabric through the machine.

Guiding Fabric Tip

You may need to lift the presser foot for heavy-weight or slippery fabrics. Hold the fabric lightly as you begin and use your hands to guide the fabric as you sew.

Securing Thread Chains

It's important to secure thread chains at the ends of each seam to prevent raveling. Use seam sealant or a threading tool for this task.

Securing With Sealant

Knot the chain at the end of the seam. Apply a drop of seam sealant to the knot and let it dry (Figure 5). Trim the ends of the thread chain. If necessary, remove excess sealant with rubbing alcohol.

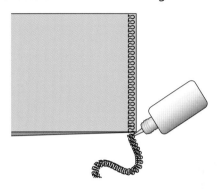

Figure 5

Securing With a Double-Eyed or Tapestry Needle

Guide the thread chain through one eye of the double-eyed needle or through the eye of a tapestry needle. Slide needle and thread chain under the looper threads (Figure 6a). Trim the ends of the thread chain.

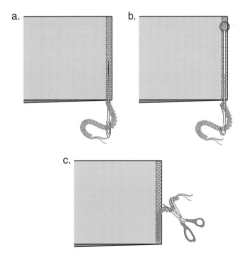

Figure 6

Securing With a Loop Turner

Insert a loop turner through the looper threads and grasp the thread chain. Pull the chain through the looper ends (Figure 6b). Trim the ends of the thread chain (Figure 6c).

Maintenance & Troubleshooting

Keeping your serger in excellent running condition is easy with regular maintenance and cleaning. However, please rely on a trained sewing machine dealer for regular checkups and service.

Maintenance

Proper care and maintenance can ensure a long, happy relationship between you and your serger. Follow these tips to keep your machine in tip-top working order:

- Unplug the serger before removing lint or performing other maintenance. Remove the throat plate and presser foot, and disengage the blades if possible.

- Clean lint and trimmed edges from the serger after each project. Use a stiff bristled brush or a mini-vac. Avoid using canned air because you may inadvertently blow lint deep into the machine.

- Clean the blades with cotton swabs and a very small amount of alcohol. After they have dried, apply a small amount of oil to the blades. Wipe off excess oil to avoid transferring it to your fabric.

- Loosen tensions completely and floss with non-waxed dental floss to remove broken threads, short fibers and lint.

- Change needles often. Dull or bent needles will adversely affect your stitching and may even tear the fabric.

- Follow the manufacturer's recommendations for how and when to oil your machine. Begin by cleaning out all visible lint. Then apply the suggested amount of oil to the moving parts.

- Have your serger professionally maintained on a regular basis. Consult with your machine dealer and/or your owner's manual regarding scheduling and servicing.

- Cover the serger when not in use. Most sergers come with a custom fit cover. Covers are also available at fabric stores and from sewing machine dealers.

Troubleshooting

Serging is fun but when you encounter problems, the fun quickly turns into frustration. When dealing with dilemmas, first check the threading and then check the tension. Refer to the following solutions for common problems:

Broken Thread
- Make sure the machine is threaded correctly with no crossed or twisted threads.

- Make sure that the thread unwinds evenly from the spool without stopping or catching.

- Reduce the tension slightly.

- Replace bent or dull needles.

- Replace old, brittle or low-quality threads.

Skipped or Irregular Stitches
- Use the proper needle. Check your owner's manual to see if a certain brand or type is recommended for your machine.

- Increase the stitch width and length when using a heavyweight fabric.

- Increase the pressure of the presser foot.

- Make sure that the thread unwinds evenly from the spool without stopping or catching.

Puckered Fabric
- Refer to your owner's manual and make adjustments to the differential feed.

- Place the stitch finger in the correct position.

- Loosen the tension on the needle or on one of the loopers.

- Decrease the presser foot pressure.

- Widen the stitch width.

Stretched Fabric
- Refer to your owner's manual and adjust the differential feed.

- Lighten the presser foot pressure and/or shorten the length of the stitch.

- Wrap the fabric edge with water-soluble stabilizer before stitching.

- Guide the fabric evenly through the serger with no stretching or pulling.

Loose Straight Stitches
- Increase the needle tension one number at a time and test stitching between each adjustment.

- Rethread the machine to ensure that the threads are set completely within the guides.

- Threading the machine while the tension is engaged will result in unbalanced stitches. Loosen the tension settings and rethread the machine.

Overcast Loops Not Aligned or Extending Past the Edge

- Adjust the looper tension settings.

- Rethread the machine to ensure that the threads are set completely within the guides.

- Adjust the cutting width setting.

Loose Rolled Edge

- Lengthen the stitch and use the smallest needle possible. These steps will reduce the number and the size of the needle holes inserted in the fabric edge.

- Wrap the fabric edge with a strip of water-soluble stabilizer before stitching.

- Provide an anchor seam for serging. Use your sewing machine to stitch a straight line along the fabric edge and serge over the stitched line.

Ragged Trimmed Edge

- Replace nicked or dull blades.

- Increase stitching speed when stitching on heavy-weight fabric.

Ragged Rolled Edge

- Use thread that will provide increased coverage, such as woolly nylon.

- Wrap the fabric edge with a strip of water-soluble stabilizer before stitching.

- Adjust the stitch to create a wider fold in the fabric edge.

Pinched Flatlock

- Reposition the fabric to allow the stitches to hang farther off the folded edge.

- Use fabric with enough body to provide a proper folded edge.

Jammed Machine

- Insert the fabric in front of the cutter and not behind it.

- Allow for the trimmed fabric to drop away from the machine rather than under the presser foot.

- Leave a long thread chain after stitching. A short tail will pull away and become caught under the presser foot. ■

Licorice Mix Strip Quilt

Small dark squares are used to add bite to this colorful composition. The patterned bands are cut from a fabric Jelly Roll, a coiled roll of precut strips. Serge the edges to keep the long strips straight and the seams secure.

Finished Size
Quilt Size: 35 x 53 inches

Serger Stitches
4-thread overlock stitch
3-thread wide overlock stitch
Chain stitch

Materials
- 1 package 2½-inch-wide precut strips (at least 40 strips)
- 2 yards 44/45-inch-wide 100 percent solid cotton*
- 38 x 54-inch rectangle double-sided fusible batting*
- Basic sewing supplies and equipment

*Sample made with black solid fabric and Fusible Warm Fleece 2™ double-sided fusible fleece from The Warm Company™.

Threads
- 4 cones coordinating all-purpose serger thread
- 1 spool 12 wt cotton thread*
- 1 spool 30 wt cotton thread*

*Sample made with Sulky 12 wt and 30 wt cotton thread.

Project Notes
Refer to Getting Started on page 4 for thread choices, stitches and general serger information.

Read through all instructions before beginning your project.

Stitch right sides together unless otherwise noted.

Be sure to test your stitches on a scrap of project fabric or similar fabric to ensure stitch perfection before beginning your project.

Cutting

From precut strips:
- Remove all selvage edges. Cut each strip into 2 (2½ x 20-inch) strips.

From solid cotton:
- Cut 3 (2½-inch by fabric width) strips. Subcut 40 (2½-inch) squares.
- Cut 2 (3-inch by fabric width) strips. Trim strips to 3 x 36-inch top and bottom borders.
- Cut 2 (3-inch by fabric width) side border strips.

Completing the Quilt Top
Serger Stitch: Set serger for 4-thread overlock stitch with all-purpose serger thread in needles and loopers.

1. Serge a 2½-inch square to one end of each 2½ x 20-inch strip (Figure 1). Do not press seams.

20"   2½"

Figure 1

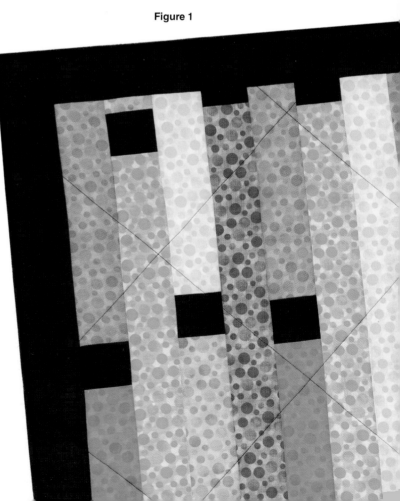

2. Serge square/strip units end to end to make one long strip (Figure 2).

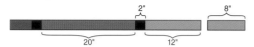

Figure 2

3. Trim 8 inches from one end of the long strip referring again to Figure 2.

4. Fold and cut long strip in half. Serge the resulting two strips together along long edges (Figure 3). *Note: Make sure that the seams between the squares and strips all fold in the same direction while stitching.*

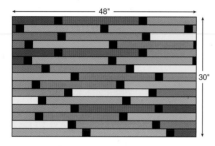

Figure 3

5. Repeat step 4 until the serged rectangle measures approximately 30 inches or 15–16 strips long (Figure 4). Trim width to 48 inches. Press all seams in same direction.

Figure 4

6. Serge 3 x 54-inch border strips to opposite long sides of quilt top. Press seams toward strips and trim to match quilt side length.

7. Serge 3 x 36-inch border strips to opposite short sides of quilt top. Press seams toward strips and trim to match quilt side length.

8. Mark diagonal lines across quilt top approximately 8 inches apart in both directions referring to Figure 5.

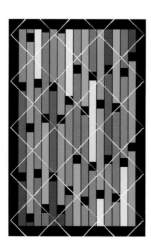

Figure 5

Completing the Quilt

1. Create a quilt sandwich by layering the quilt back, wrong side up, batting and quilt top, right side up. Fuse layers together following batting manufacturer's instructions. Trim layers even with quilt top.

Serger Stitch: Set serger for chain stitch with 30 wt cotton thread in needle and all-purpose serger thread in looper.

2. Begin serging on a fabric scrap and then onto the quilt top centering the chain stitch on a marked quilting line to quilt the layers together.

3. Serge along line and off quilt onto a fabric scrap. Cut fabric scraps away from ends of chain stitching. Apply seam sealant to both ends of seam.

4. Serge along each quilting line separately. Roll up the quilt as needed to fit into the serger throat area to stitch all quilting lines.

Serger Stitch: Set serger for 3-thread wide overlock stitch with 12 wt cotton thread in upper looper. Use left needle only. Thread all-purpose serger thread in left needle and lower looper. Refer to manual to set a wide stitch width and shorten stitch length to stitch a satin-stitch–looking stitch.

5. Serge the opposite long sides first, serging off the ends. Then serge the top and bottom edges of the quilt, again serging off the ends.

6. Secure thread chains in seam allowances to complete. ■

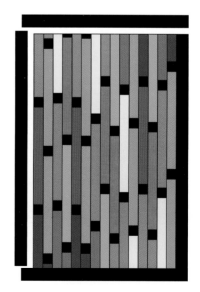

Licorice Mix Strip Quilt
Assembly Diagram 35" x 53"

Sweet Dreams Pillowcase

Dreaming of airplanes, elephants or palm trees? Trade plain white for a lively print and dream in living color with a serged-edge pillowcase that is sturdy and washable.

Finished Size
Standard pillowcase

Serger Stitches
4-thread overlock stitch

Materials
Materials listed make 1 standard pillowcase.

- 44/45-inch-wide 100 percent cotton:
  ⅛ yard contrasting solid or tonal
  ⅓ yard coordinating tonal
  ¾ yard print
- Basic sewing supplies and equipment

Threads
- 4 cones coordinating all-purpose serger thread

Project Notes
Refer to Getting Started on page 4 for thread choices, stitches and general serger information.

Read through all instructions before beginning your project.

Stitch with right sides together unless otherwise noted.

Be sure to test your stitches on a scrap of project fabric or similar fabric to ensure stitch perfection before beginning your project.

Cutting

From contrasting solid or tonal:
- Cut 1 (1½ x 44-inch) strip for band trim.

From coordinating tonal:
- Cut 1 (10 x 43-inch) rectangle for pillowcase band.

From print:
- Cut 1 (27 x 43-inch) rectangle for pillowcase.

Assembly
Serger Stitch: Set serger for 4-thread overlock stitch with all-purpose serger thread in needles and loopers for all construction.

1. Fold and press band trim in half lengthwise.

2. Position band on right side of pillowcase matching long raw edges (Figure 1).

Figure 1

3. Position pillowcase right sides together on the trim and band unit matching the long raw edges (Figure 2). Pin in place.

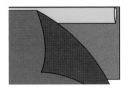

Figure 2

4. Roll the pillowcase toward the trim/band referring to Figure 3a.

5. Pull the band up and over the rolled pillowcase, matching raw edges of band, trim and one side of the pillowcase. Refer to Figure 3b. Repin through all layers.

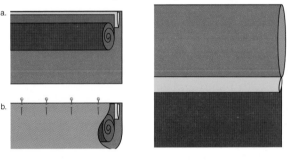

Figure 3   **Figure 4**

6. Serge through all layers. Turn right side out and press band and trim away from pillowcase (Figure 4).

7. Fold and pin pillowcase in half right sides together matching raw side edges and band seams. Serge side seam closed.

8. To create a crisp corner at pillowcase top edge; fold the side seam to one side (Figure 5a) and pin in place.

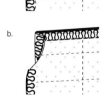

Figure 5

9. Serge the pillowcase top raw edge (Figure 5b). Secure the thread chains.

10. Turn pillowcase right side out and press seams flat. ■

Ribbon Weave T-Shirt

A little texture goes a long way when applied to a plain T-shirt. Use your serger to embed the dark threads, then weave in contrasting ribbon and call it a success!

Finished Size
Your size

Serger Stitches
4-thread overlock stitch
2-thread wide flatlock stitch

Materials
- 1 T-shirt, your size
- 1 yard nonwoven fusible interfacing
- 2 contrasting colors ⅛-inch-wide ribbon:
    3 yards each (ribbon colors should contrast with T-shirt and with each other)
- Size 90/14 needle
- Basic sewing supplies and equipment

Threads
- 4 cones coordinating all-purpose serger thread
- 1 spool 12 wt cotton contrasting thread*

*Sample made with Sulky 12 wt cotton thread.

Project Notes
Refer to Getting Started on page 4 for thread choices, stitches and general serger information.

Read through all instructions before beginning your project.

Stitch right sides together unless otherwise noted. Be sure to test your stitches on a scrap of project fabric or similar fabric to ensure stitch perfection before beginning your project.

Cutting

From nonwoven fusible interfacing:
- Cut 3 (¾ x 27-inch) strips.

Assembly
Serger Stitch: Set serger for 2-thread wide flatlock stitch at widest width referring to manual. Insert 90/14 needle as left needle; remove right needle. Thread 12 wt cotton thread into left needle and all-purpose serger thread in looper.

1. Turn T-shirt wrong side out. Mark three angled lines across shirt front between the armhole seams referring to Figure 1.

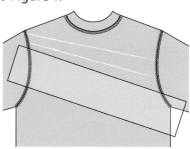

Figure 1

2. Release armhole seams where lines intersect, plus 1½ inches above and below.

3. Center and fuse interfacing strips on marked lines following manufacturer's instructions.

4. Fold along marked lines and pin in place.

5. Position folded edge under presser foot with folded edge about halfway between left needle and trimming knife. **Do not cut fold while stitching.**

6. Serge along fold. Stitches will extend slightly beyond the fold (Figure 2).

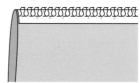

Figure 2

7. Carefully pull the seam open and flat to expose the ladder on the right side of the T-shirt.

8. Weave two contrasting ribbon lengths through the ladder of the flatlock stitch on the right side of the T-shirt referring to photo.

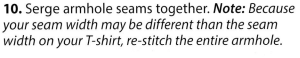

9. Repeat steps 4–8 to make three angled woven embellishments. To secure the ribbon, use an all-purpose sewing machine to stitch across ribbon ends close to the fabric edge. If a sewing machine is not available, hand-stitch the ribbon ends to the fabric edge. Trim ribbon ends (Figure 3).

Figure 3

Serger Stitch: Set serger for 4-thread overlock stitch with all-purpose serger thread in needles and loopers.

10. Serge armhole seams together. *Note: Because your seam width may be different than the seam width on your T-shirt, re-stitch the entire armhole.*

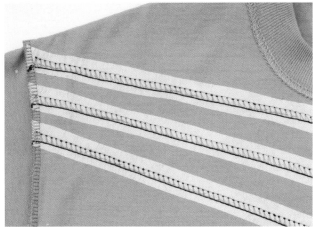

11. Secure thread chains in seam. ■

Upscale T-Shirt

Ribbing is the hallmark of a standard T-shirt. Discard it for a classic rounded neck and your boring tee is now surprisingly sophisticated.

Finished Size
Your size

Serger Stitches
3-thread wide overlock stitch
Wide cover stitch

Materials
- 1 ribbed-neck T-shirt, your size
- ¾ yard (1-inch-wide) fine fusible knit interfacing*
- Basic sewing supplies and equipment

Sample made with SewKeysE Extremely Fine 1-inch-wide Fusible Knit Interfacing.

Threads
- 3 cones coordinating all-purpose serger thread

Project Notes
Refer to Getting Started on page 4 for thread choices, stitches and general serger information.

Read through all instructions before beginning your project.

Stitch right sides together unless otherwise noted.

Be sure to test your stitches on a scrap of project fabric or similar fabric to ensure stitch perfection before beginning your project.

Altering Neckline
Serger Stitch: Set serger for 3-thread 7mm-wide overlock stitch with all-purpose serger thread in needles and loopers.

1. Trim ribbing away from T-shirt neckline. Cut close to stitching line being careful not to stretch neckline (Figure 1).

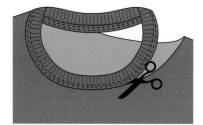

Figure 1

2. Carefully measure around neckline. Cut interfacing tape neckline measurement plus 2 inches.

3. Mark a line 2 inches from one end of interfacing tape and ⅜ inch from one long edge (Figure 2).

Figure 2

4. Make clips 1 inch apart from edge to ⅜-inch line along long edge (Figure 3). Do not clip beyond the line.

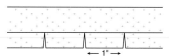

Figure 3

5. Beginning at a shoulder seam, pin the non-fusible side of the un-clipped edge of the interfacing tape to the right side of the T-shirt neckline (Figure 4). Overlap tape ends at shoulder seam.

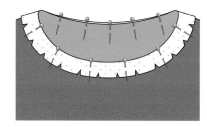

Figure 4

6. With T-shirt on bottom, serge tape to T-shirt. Skim edge with trimming knife; do not trim edge. Secure thread chains in seam.

7. Fold seam allowance and interfacing tape to wrong side and fuse in place following manufacturer's instructions.

Serger Stitch: Set serger for wide cover stitch with all-purpose serger thread referring to manual instructions.

8. With right side of presser foot butted up against the seam allowance, begin stitching a cover stitch around the neckline.

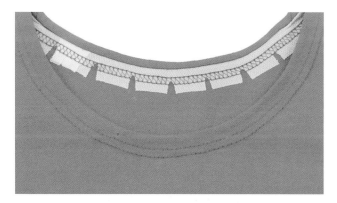

9. Serge around neckline to within 3 inches of where stitching begins. Stop stitching and trim top and bottom threads from beginning of stitching. Continue stitching overlapping the first stitches about 1 inch.

10. Raise presser foot and insert tweezers under presser foot and behind needles. Pull tweezers toward you pulling about 4 inches of thread to the front of the presser foot and cut.

11. Gently pull the T-shirt back and to the left of the presser foot, pulling the top threads to the wrong side making an invisible join on shoulder (Figure 5).

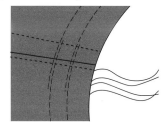

Figure 5

12. Trim looper threads and secure thread tails in seam.

Altering Hemline

Serger Stitch: Set serger for 3-thread 7mm-wide overlock stitch with all-purpose serger thread in needles and loopers.

1. Turn and press T-shirt to wrong side at determined new hemline. Pin to hold in place evenly.

2. To stitch hem, position a strip of blue painter's tape 1 inch from the left needle on the serger bed as a hem guide (Figure 6).

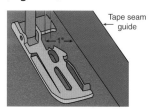

Figure 6

3. Raise presser foot. With T-shirt right side up, position hem fold against hem guide and lower presser foot referring again to Figure 6.

4. Serge around T-shirt hem overlapping stitching as done around neckline referring to steps 9–12 of Altering Neckline.

5. Press hem. Turn T-shirt wrong side out and carefully trim away excess fabric close to stitching (Figure 7). ■

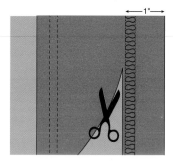

Figure 7

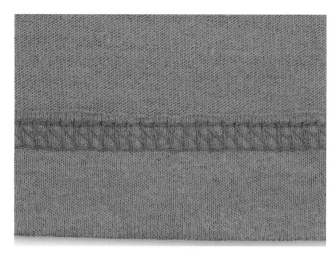

Wind & Water Throw Pillow

Can serged edges be used as a distinctive design element? Yes! These repeated rows of colorful thread bring to mind sunlit ripples in a cool pond.

Finished Size
15 x 15 inches

Serger Stitches
4-thread overlock stitch
3-thread 7mm-wide overlock stitch
Chain stitch

Materials
- 44/45-inch-wide 100 percent cotton:
    1 yard solid
- ½ yard lightweight fusible interfacing*
- 16-inch standard pillow form
- Basic sewing supplies and equipment

Sample made with Inspira® Fusible no show mesh cut-a-way stabilizer.

Threads
- 4 cones coordinating all-purpose serger thread
- 1 cone each 2 contrasting colors 12 wt cotton thread*

Sample made with Sulky 12 wt cotton serger thread.

Project Notes
Refer to Getting Started on page 4 for thread choices, stitches and general serger information.

Read through all instructions before beginning your project.

Stitch right sides together unless otherwise noted.

Be sure to test your stitches on a scrap of project fabric or similar fabric to ensure stitch perfection before beginning your project.

Cutting

From solid cotton:
- Cut 1 (24-inch by fabric width) strip.
    Subcut 1 (16 x 24-inch) pillow top rectangle.
        Set aside remainder for making pillow back.

From interfacing:
- Cut 1 (16 x 24-inch) rectangle.

Assemble Pillow Top
1. Fuse interfacing to wrong side of pillow top rectangle following manufacturer's instructions.

2. Cut 16 (1½ x 16-inch) strips from interfaced rectangle.

Serger Stitch: Set serger for 3-thread 7mm-wide overlock stitch. Thread color #1 (12 wt cotton) in upper looper, color #2 (12 wt cotton) in lower looper and regular serger thread in left needle. Shorten stitch length to stitch a satin stitch.

3. Serge two 1½-inch-wide strips right sides together lengthwise (Figure 1). Skim the edge with the cutting knife rather than cutting any of the edge.

Figure 1   **Figure 2**

4. Always begin serging from the same end so that color #1 will be on the left and color #2 will be on the right of each seam (Figure 2).

Serger Stitch: Set serger for 4-thread overlock with all-purpose serger thread in needles and loopers.

5. Serge strips together into pairs and then serge pairs together to make a pillow top approximately 16 inches long and 16 strips wide.

Serger Stitch: Set serger for chain stitch with all-purpose serger thread in needle and looper. Disengage cutting knife.

6. Mark center of pillow top perpendicular to seams (Figure 3).

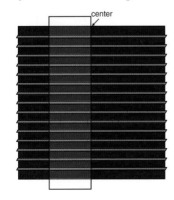

Figure 3

Making a Simple Pillow Back

1. Cut pillow back rectangles the pillow width by ⅔ of the pillow length. For example, for a 15-inch square pillow cut two rectangles 15 x 10 inches.

2. Serge along long side of one backing rectangle to finish edge. Set aside. For example, backing rectangles for an 18-inch square pillow may be cut 18 x 12 inches. Serge one of the 18-inch sides.

3. Fold and press 1 inch to wrong side of second rectangle along long side.

4. Fold again right sides together along the raw edge referring to Figure A.

Figure A

5. Serge together second folded edge and raw edge to create a hem. Press serged seam allowance away from hem (Figure B).

Figure B

6. Layer and pin hemmed backing rectangle right sides together matching raw edges of bottom half of pillow top. Layer and pin set-aside backing rectangle right sides together matching raw edges of top half of pillow top and overlapping first rectangle referring to Figure C.

Figure C

7. Stitch layers together around pillow outside edges as instructed in pattern to complete pillow back.

7. Mark topstitching lines 2½ inches apart from center of pillow referring to Figure 4.

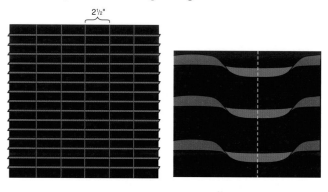

2½"

Figure 4   **Figure 5**

8. Chain-stitch down center line allowing the seams to fold down in front of the presser foot (Figure 5). Topstitch the seams down in the opposite direction every other stitching line.

9. Trim topstitched pillow top to a square. Add seam sealant to seam ends after trimming. ***Note:*** *Sample was trimmed to 15 inches square.*

Completing Pillow

Serger Stitch: Set serger for 4-thread overlock with all-purpose serger thread in needles and loopers. Re-engage cutting knife.

1. Cut and prepare pillow backs and attach to pillow top referring to Making a Simple Pillow Back (at left).

2. To make sharp corners, stitch off the corners as indicated. Fold the seam allowance to back side (Figure 6a).

a.

3. Continue stitching next side of pillow stitching folded seam in place (Figure 6b).

b.

4. Secure thread tails at seam ends.

Figure 6

5. Turn pillow right side out; press.

6. Insert pillow form. ***Note:*** *For a plump look, use a pillow form 1–2 inches larger than the overall size of your completed pillow.* ■

Take-a-Bow Tree Skirt

The versatility of serger sewing is on display with this timeless tree skirt. A serger can piece together straight seams as well as a sewing machine can, and as a bonus it will finish and trim all fabric edges.

Finished Size
Approximately 54-inch diameter

Serger Stitches
4-thread overlock stitch
Chain stitch (optional)

Materials
- 44/45-inch-wide 100 percent cotton:
    1 yard coordinating tonal for outside border
    1 yard coordinating tonal for middle border
    1¼ yards coordinating print for center
- 5½ yards (20-inch-wide) lightweight fusible nonwoven interfacing*
- Hex N More ruler*
- Basic sewing supplies and equipment

*Sample made with 911F Pellon® Fusible interfacing and Hex N More ruler manufactured by Jaybird Quilts and available through AnniesCatalog.com.

Threads
- 4 cones all-purpose serger thread coordinating with outside border

Project Notes
Refer to Getting Started on page 4 for thread choices, stitches and general serger information.

Read through all instructions before beginning your project.

Stitch right sides together unless otherwise noted.

Be sure to test your stitches on a scrap of project fabric or similar fabric to ensure stitch perfection before beginning your project.

Cutting
Before cutting, fuse interfacing to the wrong side of all fabrics following manufacturer's directions.

From outside border tonal:
- Cut 6 (5-inch by fabric width) strips.
    Trim strips to 5 x 29 inches for outside border.
- Cut 1 (2-inch by fabric width) strip.
    Trim strip to 2 x 36 inches for center hole trim.

From middle border tonal:
- Cut 6 (5½-inch by fabric width) strips.
    Trim strips to 5½ x 29 inches for middle border.

From center print:
- Cut 6 (20-inch sided) equilateral triangles using the Hex N More ruler following manufacturer's instructions.

Assembly
Serger Stitch: Set serger for 4-thread overlock stitch with all-purpose serger thread in needles and loopers.

1. Mark the centers of one side of each triangle and each 5½-inch-wide middle border strip (Figure 1).

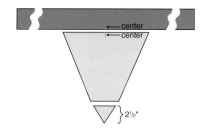

Figure 1

2. Mark the triangle point opposite the marked side 2½ inches from the point. Trim off straight referring again to Figure 1.

3. With border strip on bottom, match center marks and raw edges and serge border strip to triangle (Figure 2). Apply seam sealant to seam at edges of triangle. Press seam toward darker fabric.

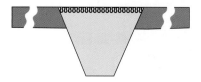

Figure 2

4. Serge 5-inch-wide outside border to middle border right sides together matching center marks and raw edges.

5. Press 2 x 36-inch center hole trim in half wrong sides together lengthwise. Cut into six 1 x 6-inch pieces.

6. Pin and serge a strip to the right side of the triangle trimmed point matching raw edges; press toward strip.

7. Trim borders and center hole trim even with triangle sides referring to Figure 3.

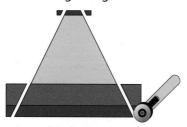

Figure 3

8. Repeat steps 1–7 to make six bordered triangles.

9. Pin and serge triangles right sides together matching seams (Figure 4). Do not serge together first and last triangles in tree skirt. Serge raw edges of first and last triangles to finish.

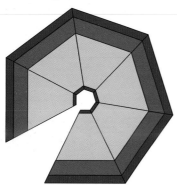

Figure 4

10. Secure thread chains on both ends of all seams. Press seams to one side (Figure 5a).

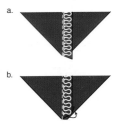

Figure 5

11. Fold seam ends back under themselves at each corner and pin in place referring to Figure 5b.

12. Press and pin finished edges of opening between the sections to the wrong side to make a hem.

13. Use all-purpose sewing machine to topstitch ⅛ inch from the outside edge of the tree skirt to secure serged seam ends. ***Note:*** *If a sewing machine is not available, set serger for a 3-thread chain stitch to topstitch around the outside edge of the tree skirt.* ■

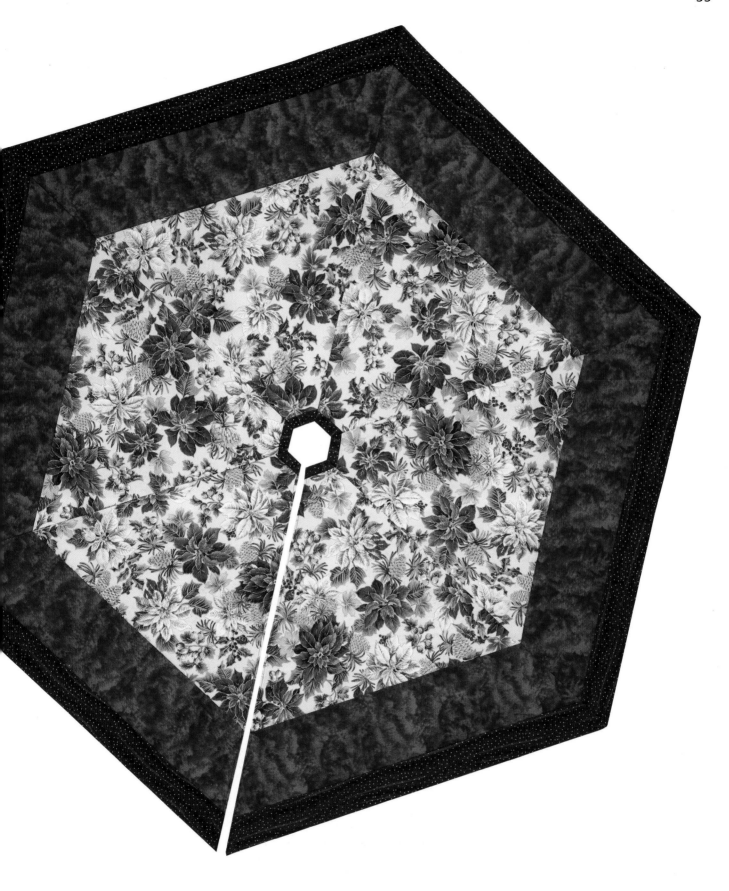

Fiesta Tiered Skirt

Celebrate the end of boring skirts with these snappy neon layers. Soft gathers and bold edges work together to make a skirt that will be the hit of any party.

Finished Size
Your size

Serger Stitches
4-thread overlock stitch
3-thread rolled edge stitch
Gathering stitch

Materials
Materials listed are for children's sizes 2–6. Adjust amounts for larger sizes. See Cutting instructions.

- 44/45-inch-wide 100 percent cotton: ½ yard each 3 coordinating prints
- 1 package 1-inch-wide elastic band
- Serger gathering foot or attachment
- Basic sewing supplies and equipment

Threads
- 4 cones coordinating all-purpose serger thread
- 1 cone black texturized thread

Project Notes
Refer to Getting Started on page 4 for thread choices, stitches and general serger information.

Read through all instructions before beginning your project.

Stitch right sides together unless otherwise noted.

Be sure to test your stitches on a scrap of project fabric or similar fabric to ensure stitch perfection before beginning your project.

Determining Your Size
Measure the waist and determine the desired finished length of the skirt referring to Figure 1.

To determine the width of the ruffle strips, divide the skirt length by 3 tiers of ruffles and add ½ inch for seams.

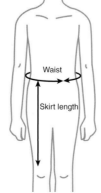

Figure 1

To determine the length of the flat bands, multiply the waist measurement by 1½.

To determine width of flat bands, subtract ½ inch from determined ruffle width.

> For example, the sample skirt was made for a 20-inch waist and a 12-inch finished skirt length.
>
> Ruffle strip length: (12 inches ÷ 3) + ½ inch = 4½ inches wide
>
> Flat band length: 20 inches x 1½ = 30 inches long.
>
> Flat band width: 4½ inches–½ inch = 4 inches wide.

Cutting

From each print fabric:
- Cut 2 (determined ruffle width x 42-inch) ruffle strips.
  For sizes larger than children's 6X you may need to cut 3 ruffle strips of each fabric. Cut enough strips to have at least twice the length of the flat band.
- Cut 1 (determined flat band width x length) flat band strip.
  For sizes larger than children's 6X you may need to cut more than 1 strip to have the determined flat band length.

From elastic:
- Cut 1 piece of elastic the waist measurement minus 1 inch.

Assembly
Serger Stitch: Set serger for 4-thread overlock stitch with all-purpose serger thread in needles and loopers.

1. Stitch same color ruffle strips right sides together along short ends to make one long strip; press seam to one side.

Serger Stitch: Set serger for 3-thread rolled edge stitch. Use black texturized thread in the upper looper and all-purpose serger thread in the needle and lower looper.

2. Serge a rolled edge stitch along one long edge of each ruffle strip to hem ruffle.

Serger Stitch: Attach the gathering foot to your machine referring to your manual. Set serger for 4-thread overlock stitch with all-purpose serger thread in needles and loopers. Refer to your machine manual to adjust the differential feed and stitch length to create the desired ruffle fullness.

3. With raw edges and right sides together, position the flat band on the ruffle strip matching short ends. Serge and gather the long raw edges together (Figure 2). *Note: The ruffle strip will be longer than the flat band.*

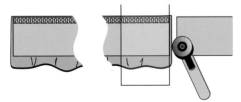

Figure 2

4. Apply seam sealant to the end of the flat band/ruffle seam and to the rolled edge hem directly below it. Let dry.

5. Trim the ruffle even with the flat band referring again to Figure 2.

6. Repeat steps 1–5 with all same color ruffle/flat band units.

Serger Stitch: Set serger for 4-thread overlock stitch with all-purpose serger thread in needles and loopers for the rest of skirt construction.

7. Fold desired flat band/ruffle unit right sides together along the seam. Position and pin on the right side of the bottom flat band/ruffle unit matching the seam to the raw edge (Figure 3).

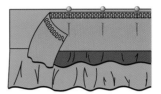

Figure 3

8. Serge through all layers. Trim no more than ⅛ inch from the seam with the serger blades.

9. Repeat steps 7 and 8 to add all flat band/ruffle units.

10. To create a waistline casing, fold and press the raw edge of top flat band/ruffle unit 1½ inches to the wrong side of the skirt (Figure 4).

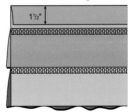

Figure 4

11. Fold the folded edge 1½ inches to the right side of the skirt with the raw edge and the folded edge even (Figure 5). Pin in place and serge. Press seam away from the casing. *Note: This seam will be close but not overlap the top flat band/ruffle unit seam.*

Figure 5

12. Thread the elastic through the casing and align each end with the raw edges of the casing. Pin both ends of the elastic 2 inches in from the raw edges of the casing to secure. Distribute the fabric gathers evenly along the waistband.

13. Fold the skirt in half right sides together and pin center back seam together matching flat band/ruffle raw edges, rolled hem edges and seams (Figure 6).

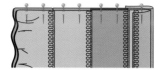

Figure 6

14. Serge through all layers, beginning at the bottom rolled edge hem. As you stitch, remove pins before they reach the cutting blade to avoid damaging the needles or blades.

15. Secure thread chains at both ends of the center back seam.

16. Pin the seam allowance to one side at the waistband and stitch in place using an all-purpose sewing machine (Figure 7). ■

Figure 7

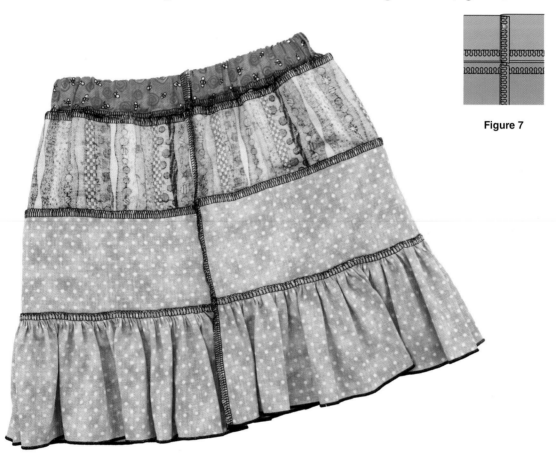

Tumbled Nine-Patch Throw Pillow

Start with a standard nine-patch. Then snip and twist to create a compelling square. Add pieced piping and get an "A" in pillow geometry.

Finished Size
15 x 15 inches

Serger Stitches
4-thread overlock stitch
3-thread overlock stitch

Materials
- 3 coordinating fat quarters solid, print or tonal
- 44/45-inch-wide 100 percent cotton:
    ⅝ yard coordinating solid, print or tonal
- 2⅓ yards cording (refer to piping foot manufacturer's instructions for correct width)
- 16-inch square pillow form
- Serger piping foot
- Basic sewing supplies and equipment

Threads
- 4 cones coordinating all-purpose serger thread

Project Notes
Refer to Getting Started on page 4 for thread choices, stitches and general serger information.

Read through all instructions before beginning your project.

Stitch right sides together unless otherwise noted.

Be sure to test your stitches on a scrap of project fabric or similar fabric to ensure stitch perfection before beginning your project.

Cutting

From fat quarter 1:
- Cut 2 (2 x 42-inch) strips. Set aside for piping.
- Cut 2 (6 x 22-inch) strips.
    Subcut 4 (6-inch) squares for pillow front.

From fat quarter 2:
- Cut 2 (2 x 42-inch) strips. Set aside for piping.
- Cut 2 (6 x 22-inch) strips.
    Subcut 4 (6-inch) squares for pillow front.

From fat quarter 3:
- Cut 2 (2 x 42-inch) strips. Set aside for piping.
- Cut 1 (6 x 22-inch) strip.
    Subcut 1 (6-inch) square for pillow front.

From coordinating yardage:
- Cut 2 (18 x 12-inch) rectangles for pillow back.

Assemble Pillow Top
Serger Stitch: Set serger for 4-thread overlock stitch with all-purpose serger thread in needles and loopers and regular serger foot.

1. Arrange the nine 6-inch squares with fat quarter 3 square at center. Serge squares together in rows. Press seams in opposite directions between rows referring to arrows in Figure 1.

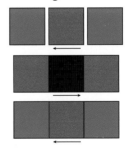

Figure 1

2. Serge rows together referring again to Figure 1 matching seams; press seams in one direction completing the pillow front.

3. Mark and cut along the horizontal and vertical center lines dividing the pillow front into quarters (Figure 2).

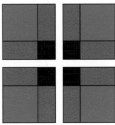

Figure 2

4. Arrange the quarters referring to Figure 3 and serge together in rows; press seams in opposite directions. Serge rows together, matching seams to complete the pillow top; press seam to one side.

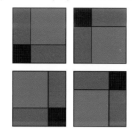

Figure 3

Making Pillow Piping

1. Serge 2 x 22-inch strips together lengthwise; press seams in same direction.

2. Cut pieced strip into 2-inch-wide strips (Figure 4). Stitch together on short ends to make one long strip for piping; press seams in one direction.

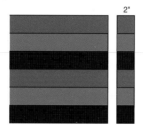

2"

Figure 4

Serger Stitch: Set serger for 3-thread overlock stitch using right needle only for 7mm width with all-purpose serger thread in needle and looper. Refer to manual to attach the piping foot.

3. Beginning approximately 2½ inches from the end of the cord, wrap the piping strip made in steps 1 and 2 around the cord end (Figure 5).

2½"

Figure 5

4. Position the cord under the piping presser foot referring to foot user instructions and serger manual, and serge along strip edges wrapping the cord. *Note: Fabric will be just under the presser foot.*

5. Pin the serged piping edge along the outside edge of the pillow top. Begin at center of one side and fold piping back at beginning and end to join the piping (Figure 6). ***Note:*** *To make it easier to keep the joined ends in place, hand-baste them to the pillow top to secure. Remove basting after serging is completed.*

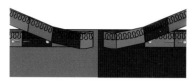

Figure 6

6. Pinch piping at corners and clip seam allowance to go around corner (Figure 7). Use a drop of seam sealant on clip to keep from fraying.

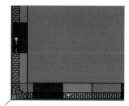

Figure 7

7. Begin serging slightly beyond the center point where the piping ends meet. With the presser foot up, slide the pillow top edge under the piping presser foot with the piping in the foot groove. Lower the foot and serge the edge, stitching off the corner.

8. Raise the presser foot, rotate the pillow top and position the piping under the presser foot groove. Place a folded piece of cardboard under the foot behind the needle to elevate the back of the presser foot, making it even with the front, and lower the foot to continue sergering. Repeat for all corners.

9. Stop serging when approximately 2 inches from the piping join and trim piping ends even with seam allowance. Continue serging over the join while holding in place.

Completing Pillow

Serger Stitch: Set serger for 7mm-wide, 4-thread overlock stitch with all-purpose serger thread in needles and loopers and piping foot.

1. Prepare and pin pillow back to top referring to Making a Simple Pillow Back on page 28.

2. With pillow top on top, raise piping presser foot and position piping under the foot groove. Lower

presser foot and serge around pillow edges to stitch around corners referring to steps 7–9 of Making Pillow Piping. Secure thread chains at seam ends.

3. Turn pillow right side out; press.

4. Insert pillow form. ***Note:*** *For a plump look, use a pillow form 1–2 inches larger than the overall size of your completed pillow.* ■

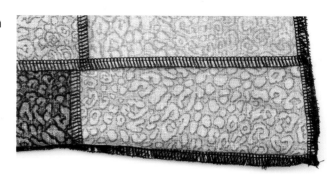

Stipple-Chic Clutch

This handy clutch can be stashed inside a drawer or tucked away in a suitcase, but don't keep it hidden. The classic styling and ready zippered top make it a go-to fashion accessory.

Finished Size
13 x 8 x 2 inches

Serger Stitches
4-thread overlock stitch
3-thread 7mm-wide overlock stitch

Materials
Note: Sample made with 100 percent cotton but any woven will work. Choose a medium- to heavy-weight woven print and a light- to medium-weight woven solid.

- 44/45-inch-wide woven:
    ½ yard print
    ½ yard light color solid
- 1 (22-inch) standard nylon zipper
- 6-inch piece ⅛-inch-wide ribbon
- Piping presser foot
- Basic sewing supplies and equipment

Threads
- 4 cones coordinating all-purpose serger thread

Project Notes
Refer to Getting Started on page 4 for thread choices, stitches and general serger information.

Read through all instructions before beginning your project.

Stitch right sides together unless otherwise noted.

Be sure to test your stitches on a scrap of project fabric or similar fabric to ensure stitch perfection before beginning your project.

Cutting

From print:
- Cut 1 (14 x 20-inch) rectangle for clutch outside.

From light color solid:
- Cut 1 (14 x 20-inch) rectangle for clutch lining.

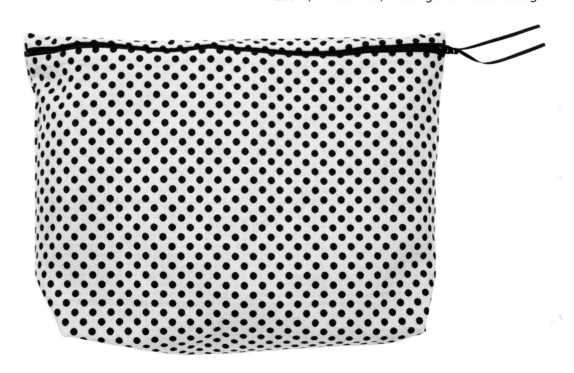

Assembly

Serger Stitch: Set serger for 3-thread 7mm-wide overlock stitch with all-purpose serger thread in needle and looper. Use right needle only. Refer to your machine manual to attach piping presser foot.

1. Mark a line 2 inches from zipper top and a second line 2 inches from that (Figure 1a).

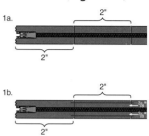

Figure 1

2. Mark lines ⅜ inch from either side of the zipper teeth referring to Figure 1b.

3. Trim away zipper tape cutting on marked lines referring to Figure 2 on page 9 and Trimming Tips in Getting Started on page 7.

Figure 2

4. Position zipper between the right sides of the clutch outside and lining fabrics with notch edge at edge of fabric and matching zipper tape to raw edges (Figure 3). Pin in place and unzip zipper.

Figure 3

5. Raise presser foot with needle in highest position. Position zipper notch to the left of the presser foot and slide zipper teeth under foot into piping foot groove (Figure 4).

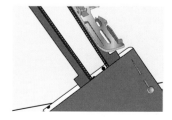

Figure 4

6. Lower presser foot and serge through all layers. When close to the end of the zipper, gently curve zipper end to the left and serge off the zipper. Do not serge over the zipper pull.

7. Close zipper and press fabrics away from zipper teeth (Figure 5).

Figure 5

8. Referring to steps 4–6 and Figure 6, position zipper between the right sides of the opposite 14-inch edge of the clutch outside and lining fabrics. Turn fabric right side out and press fabric away from zipper teeth.

Figure 6

9. Turn clutch lining side out and lay flat with zipper at center of clutch. Measure and pin mark ½ inch away from zipper through top two layers. Fold clutch in half outside sides together at ½-inch mark and pin in place to hold (Figure 7).

Figure 7

10. Mark 1 inch up from bottom fold on both sides of folded clutch referring to Figure 8.

Figure 8

11. Open bottom flat. Keeping lining and outside fabrics together, fold the bottom together matching the lines to make a pleat in the bottom of the clutch (Figure 9). Pin to secure pleat in place.

Figure 9

12. Pin sides together, mark and straighten evenly; trim zipper ends even with sides (Figure 10). Open zipper approximately 4 inches.

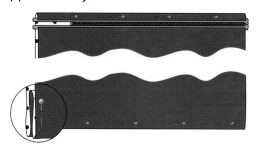

Figure 10

Serger Stitch: Set serger for 4-thread overlock stitch with all-purpose serger thread in needles and loopers. Attach standard presser foot following manual instructions.

13. Serge side seams together slowly hand-walking the serger across the zipper teeth to avoid breaking a needle.

14. Secure thread chains at both ends of the side seams.

15. With all purpose sewing machine, straight-stitch across the zipper teeth to reinforce side seam.

16. Turn clutch right side out. Bottom will form a triangle at corners (Figure 11). ◼

Figure 11

Fabric & Supplies

The following materials were used to construct the projects in this book and are available from the companies listed at your local fabric store or Annie's Quilt & Sew catalog at AnniesCatalog.com.

Notions

- 12wt and 30wt cotton thread from Sulky® (www.sulky.com)
- Polyarn™ texturized polyester serger thread from Superior® Threads (www.superiorthreads.com)
- 1-inch-wide Extremely Fine Double Sided Fusible Stay Tape (Item #039) from SewKeysE by Emma Seabrooke (www.emmaseabrooke.com)
- Inspira® Fusible "No Show" Mesh cutaway stabilizer from Husqvarna (www.husqvarnaviking.com)
- 911F Pellon® Fusible Featherweight interfacing (www.shoppellon.com)
- Hex N More ruler by Jaybird Quilts (AnniesCatalog.com)
- Fusible Warm Fleece 2™ double-sided fusible fleece from The Warm™ Company (www.warmcompany.com)

Fabric Collections

Sweet Dreams Pillowcase, page 20
Junior Pilots collection by Nancy Vasilchik for Exclusively Quilters Fabrics

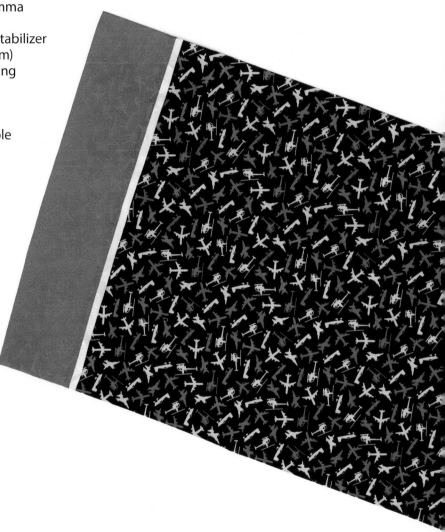

Photo Index

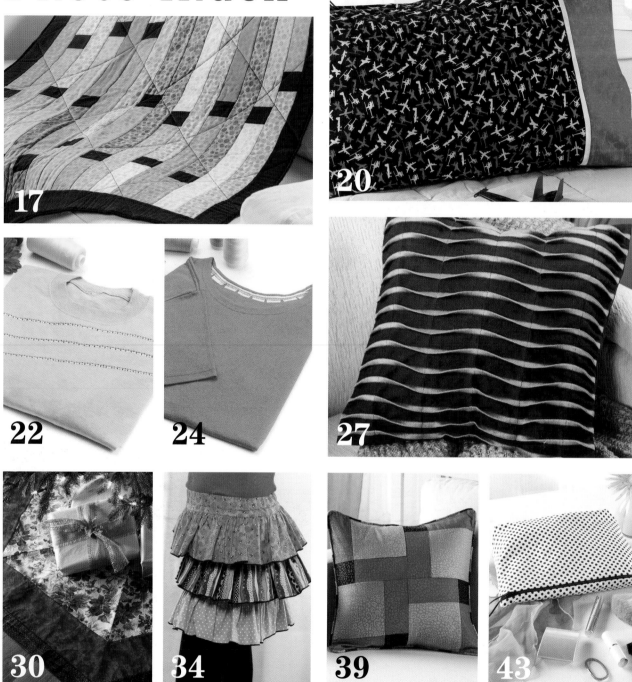

17

20

22

24

27

30

34

39

43

Annie's® *Learn Simple Serging* is published by Annie's, 306 East Parr Road, Berne, IN 46711. Printed in USA. Copyright © 2014 Annie's. All rights reserved. This publication may not be reproduced in part or in whole without written permission from the publisher.

Every effort has been made to ensure that the instructions in this pattern book are complete and accurate. We cannot, however, take responsibility for human error, typographical mistakes or variations in individual work. Please visit AnniesCustomerCare.com to check for pattern updates.

ISBN: 978-1-57367-471-3

1 2 3 4 5 6 7 8 9